T5-CCN-651

by Tyler Hansbrook
illustrated by Damian Ward

SCHOOL PUBLISHERS

Printed in China

ISBN 10: 0-15-350012-3
ISBN 13: 978-0-15-350012-1

Ordering Options
ISBN 10: 0-15-349938-9 (Grade 3 ELL Collection)
ISBN 13: 978-0-15-349938-8 (Grade 3 ELL Collection)
ISBN 10: 0-15-357251-5 (package of 5)
ISBN 13: 978-0-15-357251-7 (package of 5)

1 2 3 4 5 6 7 8 9 10 985 12 11 10 09 08 07 06

"You'd better pick those up," Elena said. She pointed to the tiny cars on the floor.

"I am still playing with them," Victor said.

"Well, you can't leave toys on the floor anymore," Elena said. "Babies pick things up and try to eat them."

Mom had just had a baby. Mom and the baby were coming home from the hospital today.

"He cannot crawl on the floor yet," said Victor.

"You should get used to being careful now," Elena said. "Everything changes when a baby comes. That is what happened when you came."

"You are only two years older than I am!" said Victor. "You do not remember."

"Oh, yes, I do," said Elena. "Mom and Dad were busy all the time. You cried a lot. I never had any fun. That is going to happen again."

"That is not true!" Victor said.

"Yes, it is!" shouted Elena.

Grandma walked into the room. "What is going on?" she asked.

"Elena says that when the baby comes we are never going to have any fun. She says that Mom and Dad will not have time for us," said Victor.

Grandma smiled. "Elena sounds like quite the expert," Grandma said.

"It is true," said Elena. "Babies take up time, and they make a lot of noise. They're everyone's favorite because they're little. Older kids do not matter as much when there is a new baby."

Grandma patted the sofa. "Come sit with me," she said.

Elena jumped up next to Grandma. Victor tried to squeeze in between them.

"It is true that babies need a lot of care," said Grandma.

"However," Grandma said, "your Mom and Dad will still have plenty of time for you."

"How do you know?" asked Victor.

"I am an expert," said Grandma. "I had baby brothers and a little sister. I had four children, so most of my children had baby brothers and sisters, too."

"I still think a baby is going to be trouble," said Elena.

"Sometimes they are," said Grandma, "but babies also can be very interesting. You will be able to watch your new baby brother grow and learn. You can even teach him things."

"I think it's going to be fun to have a baby brother," said Victor. "There will be one more person to play with me. Also, I will not be the youngest one in the family."

Suddenly, they heard the front door open.

"Mom and Dad and the baby are here!" cried Victor.

Elena, Victor, and Grandma hurried to the door. Mom walked in, followed by Mom. Dad was carefully carrying the baby.

"Please, let me see the baby!" Victor said right away.

Mom pulled aside the blanket. The baby immediately began to cry.

"I told you," said Elena.

Elena looked at the baby. Suddenly, the baby stopped crying. He reached up with a tiny hand. Elena looked at her new baby brother. He smiled, and she smiled, too.

"Hello, baby," she said in a soft voice. "He likes me. I told you having a baby brother would be great!"

Scaffolded Language Development

PRONOUNS Remind students that pronouns are words that can take the place of nouns. Point out examples in the book. Then model an example of changing a noun to a pronoun: *Elena looked at the baby* becomes: *She looked at the baby*. Have students chorally read each sentence below and then read it again using the appropriate pronoun in place of the underlined subject.

1. <u>Victor</u> is excited to get a new brother.
2. <u>Grandma</u> makes Victor and Elena feel better.
3. <u>Elena</u> holds the baby.
4. <u>Mom and Dad</u> are proud of all their children.

🌐 Social Studies

What's in a Community? Explain to students that babies are usually born at hospitals. A hospital is an important place in a community. What other places are important parts of a community? Help students make a list that might include a park, a library, and a police department.

School-Home Connection

Baby Stories Ask students to talk to older family members about when they were children. Did they have brothers or sisters or cousins? Were they younger or older? What do they remember about them?

Word Count: 512